CENTROSAURUS

A MOMENT IN TIME WITH

CENTROSAURUS

To ~~[struck out]~~
Hope To See You ~~[struck out]~~
Later This Year!

[signatures: Philip J. Currie, Eva Koppelhus]

Philip J. Currie, Eva Koppelhus and Jan Sovak

Feb. 12, 2007

TROODON
PRODUCTIONS INC

Centrosaurus is the third book from the series "A Moment In Time".
Other books in this series include:

Troodon by Eric Felber, Philip Currie and illustrated by Jan Sovak.

Albertosaurus by Eric Felber, Philip Currie and illustrated by Jan Sovak.

A MOMENT IN TIME* WITH CENTROSAURUS

*trade-mark of Troodon Productions Inc.

Text by Philip J. Currie and Eva Koppelhus
Illustrations by Jan Sovak
Edited by Laura Purdy Editing Services

"A MOMENT IN TIME" BOOKS ARE PUBLISHED BY
TROODON PRODUCTIONS INC., Suite 1910, 355 4th Avenue S.W.
Calgary, Alberta T2P OJ1, Canada

CREDITS

Design and cover by Aventinum, Prague
Colour separation and typesetting by Baroa, Prague
Printed and bound by Polygraf Print, Prešov
6/03/06/51-01

CANADIAN CATALOGUING IN PUBLICATION DATA

Currie, Philip J., 1949-
A moment in time with Centrosaurus

ISBN 0-9682512-2-6

1.Centrosaurus-Juvenile fiction. I. Sovak, Jan, 1953-
II. Koppelhus, Eva B. (Eva Bundgaard) III. Title.

PS8555.U698M64 1998   jC813'.54   C98-901012-0
PR9199.3.C798M64 1998

PREFACE

Imagine visiting the late Cretaceous period of history. Thousands of two and three tonne **centrosaurs**[*] are starting their northern **migration**. What an awesome spectacle these huge herds must have been.

Centrosaurus is one of the most commonly found **ceratopsians** (horned dinosaurs) of the late Cretaceous. Some of the largest dinosaur bonebeds ever found in Dinosaur Provincial Park, Alberta, Canada, contain the remains of thousands of centrosaurs. All were presumed drowned in a raging river.

Fossil sites in Alberta and Montana give us clues about dinosaur life in the Late Cretaceous period. It was information from these fossil sites that enabled us to write this book. The story, even though a work of fiction, uses the actual scientific information known about **Centrosaurus**. These facts are presented at the end of the story.

A Moment In Time With Centrosaurus is the third book of a series which focuses on the scientific facts known about specific prehistoric animals. By developing a story around the facts, we hope we can bring a moment in time to life for you.

[*] Bold face words can be found in the glossary at the end of the book.

CENTROSAURUS

Heading north

Thunder rolled over the landscape. Heavy **vegetation** along the edge of the marsh muffled the rumble. Towards the west, masses of black clouds boiled mountainously high. A flash of lightning sliced through the gloom. Overhead the sun still shone in a deep blue sky, adding more heat to the humid air. A lone ceratopsian browsed unconcerned, tilting his head and closing his narrow beak around bunches of water ferns. He straightened his great head, uprooting some plants and snapping the stalks of others. His long tongue wrapped around the mass of food and pulled it into his mouth, where strong teeth chopped it into small pieces.

The horned dinosaur was almost four years old, and was nearing his adult size. Millions of years later, his kind would be called *Centrosaurus*. But such names meant nothing to him. The right side of the crest over his neck was narrow and distorted from an injury in his youth. This distortion gave the neck shield an **asymmetrical**, twisted appearance. We will call him Twister.

Another peal of thunder... or was it something else? A new, more threatening rumble? Twister stopped to listen this time. The wind rose suddenly, noisily pushing leaves and branches away from the approaching storm. He heard yet another clap of thunder, but he could also detect the unmistakable growl of a **tyrannosaur**. Spinning around in an **adrenaline-fed** panic, Twister saw a ferocious *Daspletosaurus* charging towards him. He prepared to meet the rush of the big meat-eater as it leapt from the forest onto the soft muddy floor of the marsh. Realizing that he had failed to surprise his prey, the

Daspletosaurus slid to a stop just outside the range of Twister's long, sharply pointed nose horn.

The two animals stared at each other for a few moments. The tyrannosaur's **ominous** growls echoed the angry sounds of the approaching storm. Clouds blotted out the sun, and shadows engulfed the scene. The short-armed **predator** took one step towards the lone bull ceratopsian. In anticipation of a charge, Twister lowered his horn, raising the large crest at the back of his head. Heavy drops of water began to pelt their hides, a prelude to the sheets of wind-driven rain that could already be heard advancing through the forest. Without the advantage of surprise, the *Daspletosaurus* would be foolish to take on this great horned dinosaur alone. With a snort of frustration, the predator rotated in its tracks and pushed back into the forest. Twister's heavy brow horns sheltered his eyes from the rain as he watched the retreating hunter. Within minutes, the centrosaur was again uprooting vegetation with his sharp beak. Only his eyes betrayed a lingering wariness.

The next day dawned clear and soon the forest floor was dancing with beams of sunlight. Twister began his daily search for food. Without considering why, he turned towards the north, grazing and nibbling as he went. As the day wore on, he began to sense that he was not alone travelling through the forest. He could detect the presence of others of his kind. Before long, Twister was moving along the trail with four other young males. After months of avoiding all contact with other horned dinosaurs, these five animals had met on the trail moving north. There was something very natural about the way they came together, and each appreciated the companionship they had avoided for so long.

The five young males had almost reached their full adult size. Their horns curved gracefully over their noses, and their thick, leathery hides were unblemished. Faint splashes of color were beginning to show along the margins of each crest. As they approached their first mating season, the colors would intensify.

On their second day together, the group encountered an old bull, browsing peacefully in a clearing until it saw the young males. Without hesitation or provocation, the scarlet crested giant attacked the young centrosaurs. Although the youngsters were nearly as large as the old bull, none dared to meet the attack of the more experienced animal. Instinctively, the five animals split up, skirted safely around the clearing and reassembled farther to the north, out of sight of the lone giant.

The days were getting longer. There were now more hours of daylight than hours of dark. All through the long day, the centrosaurs walked. Something inside was pushing them north. Even after the slow sunset had painted the sky crimson, the little group continued to walk until they could no longer see where they were going. Only then would they pause in their long journey. Together they stood in a small group of trees and bushes where they stripped off leaves and young branches deep into the short night.

The next morning, they left the coastal forest and emerged onto a vast fern plain. In the distance they could see a giant herd of their own kind, moving in the same general direction. As the young males drew closer to the great herd, they could see that it was extremely varied. Unlike their own small group, the large herd included both males and females, some young and some old. There was at least one ancient bull. He was a giant individual with a flaming red crest, accented by bright canary-yellow skin on the face and throat. The red-rimmed eyes seemed small in his enormous skull, concealing his alertness. Most of the herd was composed of females of all ages. The heads of the larger females had similar markings to the male, although their colors were less intense. Their crests were shorter, and the nasal horns were lower and more strongly curved. Running amongst the adults were **juveniles** of two distinct sizes. The smallest, and most active, were all about a sixth of the length of the adults. Their legs were long, but their crests and horns were very short. These were the young that had hatched shortly before the previous migration. The second group of juveniles were yearlings. They were almost double the size of the small ones, and were easily identified by their slate-gray hides.

As the five young males approached the herd, they were ignored by most. However, the old bull came out to meet them. His actions made it very clear that they were not welcome. Unlike the juvenile males in his great herd, these five newcomers were large enough to be considered potential rivals. Pawing the ground, and shaking his massive head, the old bull dropped his nose and tore up great clumps of earth and vegetation with his horn. The young visitors were uncertain how to react. They hesitated, not understanding the actions of the bull. The old bull was infuriated by their failure to heed his warning. A barely audible rumble deep in his throat signaled the prelude to an attack. Suddenly, he charged.

The bull picked up speed and bore down on the hapless youngsters. The rumble in his throat increased in volume to a reverberating bellow. The sight of a mad bull bearing down on them jolted the centrosaurs out of their stupor. The young beasts scrambled to get out of the way. But one of the

centrosaurs at the back of the group was unable to see the charging bull. His view was blocked by the other animals. As the others leapt out of the path of the angry bull, the mass of flesh in front of the young male parted like a curtain to reveal the enraged giant. Although he was faster and more agile, there was not enough time for the young bull to get out of the way. There was a sickening crunch as the larger animal slammed into the unprotected flank of the surprised centrosaur.

The injured youngster collapsed to the ground and lay still. The old bull turned to confront the remaining intruders, but they were already disappearing into the dense vegetation at the edge of the forest. He did not follow them, but paced angrily between them and his harem. Finally his rage subsided, and he trotted after the mixed herd. As the old bull disappeared from view, the injured young male rose carefully to his feet. Breathing was painful because several ribs had been fractured, but this did not seem to slow his progress as he moved into the forest to find his companions.

Although the five males were scattered by the bull, they all continued to move in the same direction, north. By the next morning they were together again. The injured animal seemed somewhat recovered, although he gingerly avoided touching his left flank against anything. This was sometimes difficult to do because ticks and insects were a constant annoyance at this time of year. The urge to rub against something was almost overpowering. Fortunately their route took them through several rivers, and the cool waters were soothing.

By the end of the day, two more young males approached their group and were accepted without question. Sometimes the bachelor herd spread far across the fern plains, but the scent of a tyrannosaur was sufficient to force them back into a tight clump again. The occasional sight of the larger mixed herds of *Centrosaurus* stirred vague feelings in their chests and they were tempted to approach the larger groups. But all of the young males had encountered at least one **dominant** bull and did not want to experience that again. The smaller herd was able to move quickly—they were all in the prime of life, and could find food easily as long as they did not follow the swath of destruction left by one of the big herds.

Moving north, the days became longer and warmer. But the nights could still be cool. One morning there was a cold wind coming out of the north, and as the day wore on, the sun disappeared completely behind gray clouds. Patches of last winter's snow still lay in the hollows of north facing slopes. By mid-day a light drizzle was falling, mixed with a slurry of large wet snowflakes. As the wind picked up, the sleet froze on rocks and tree trunks. The ceratopsians were colder than they had ever been but they continued on their relentless northward trek.

They were driven by instinct. Over thousands of generations, their ancestors had gradually developed the best ways to survive. One way to survive is to find the highest quality food. During the summer months, high quality food was abundant in the North. So the centrosaurs continued walking into the cold. Their great nasal horns cut the wind, and their necks and shoulders were sheltered by the giant frills that extended from the backs of their skulls.

It was midnight before the snow stopped. The full moon broke through the clouds and the snow covered surfaces reflected its silvery rays. To the north, a glow on the horizon marked the position of the sun as it moved eastward towards morning. The centrosaurs now stood shivering in the ghostly light, their simple brains unable to appreciate the fierce beauty of the landscape.

Dawn arrived quickly. At this **latitude** there were few hours of darkness. As the morning sun warmed his hide, Twister thrashed a bush with his horn. The snow fell away to expose young, lime-green leaves. The centrosaur soon reduced the foliage to a pulp with his sharp edged rows of teeth. Within minutes, the others in the group were also feeding.

By the time the group started to move north again, melting snow was dripping from the plants and collecting into pools and rivulets. The cold night had done little harm to the plants, and the moisture was badly needed in this dry region between coastline and mountains. A rainbow of colorful flowers was in bloom. Here in the North, summer was brief. Plants had to grow quickly in order to flower and produce seeds before the winter snows arrived again. For a few short months, the region was covered with fresh growth and beautiful blooms — a feast for the animals that fed on them.

Summer

One day, the ceratopsians topped a ridge and looked down onto an extensive area rimmed by the northern sea. The vegetation was lush although most of the larger trees were spread out, giving the low-angled sunlight a chance to reach the ground. The centrosaurs had arrived at the summer feeding grounds.

Water glinted in the marshes and swamps, promising refuge from the black clouds of tiny insects that followed the herd. Although their hides were thick enough to protect most of

the body, the insects clustered around the edges of eyes, nasal openings, and even flew into ear passages. The tiniest flies were the worst, nearly driving the ceratopsians crazy with the noise in their ears. The centrosaurs breathed in thousands of the biting flies through their huge nasal openings. Here most of the bugs became stuck in the mucous that lined the nasal passages. But many insects were successful in biting the thin skin of the eyes, nose and ears. In fact, the eyelids of some of the centrosaurs were swollen to the point that the eyes were almost closed.

Other insects bored into the hides of the horned dinosaurs. These pests were usually kept under control by beautiful white birds that spent part of every day perched on the backs of their distant cousins. With their long, sharp beaks, they picked off most of the insects before they had a chance to disappear under the skin. Sometimes the birds even probed gently into open sores to pull out fat larvae of the insects that had succeeded in breaking through the skin.

The great herds dispersed into their summer pastures, and within a few days had spread throughout the region in small groups. Life was nearly perfect here. Few predators had followed them this far north. Many of the larger hunters had stopped along the way to lay their eggs and raise their young. There were **troodontids**, **velociraptors** and other small predators, but they were mostly interested in eating the smaller **mammals** and birds that were abundant here.

The sun never set at this time of the year, and the air was warm and humid. Wallowing in the water and mud of the marshlands, the ceratopsians ate almost constantly. The juveniles grew rapidly under these conditions, and the folds in the hides of the adults became smooth as they bulked out.

Twister was growing too and soon became larger than some of the males who had chased him away only a few months earlier. His nasal horn grew long and elegant, the end tapering to a sharp tip. The crest grew faster than the rest of his body, and now extended over his shoulders. A large, gnarly horn curved forward from the normal side of his crest. There was a horn on the twisted side as well, but it had not grown properly and was short and stunted. The colors intensified on his face and crest, even on the side that had been damaged in his youth.

The days became hotter and hotter, but they soon began to grow shorter as well. Each evening the sun dipped a little lower, coming closer and closer to sunset. The change was almost **imperceptible** at first, especially when the sky was cloudy. But eventually, the division between one day and the next became marked by a period of twilight when there was no sun at all. The sunsets, often crimson red, lasted for hours as the sun barely skimmed the surface of the horizon. There was a chill in the air whenever the sun disappeared. There could be no doubt that summer was ending.

As the days grew shorter, the animals' behavior began to change too. Small groups of hadrosaurs travelled past the ceratopsians ever more frequently, sometimes with young, sometimes followed by small groups of **carnivores**. Flocks of birds began practicing their flight formations, partly to exercise the wings of the young and partly to enforce discipline.

The recently hatched horned dinosaurs had grown quickly. Still, they were only a quarter of the height of their mothers. But their legs were long, and they galloped circles around the larger animals. Soon, the young animals would need all their strength and energy.

Over the course of the summer, the head of the herd had seemed to lose interest in his charges. He often wandered off to feed by himself. But one morning, this relaxed behavior suddenly changed. He rose from the ground where he had been lying, and let out a series of deep throated, powerful bellows. The older females seemed to understand. They began to move purposefully towards the south, their young following. Most of the younger females followed the loose-knit column. The southern migration had begun.

The long journey

The bull watched his harem and their young with obvious irritation. Once the main part of the column had passed, he strutted behind the stragglers, bellowing constantly. One female seemed more interested in eating than in keeping up with the others. The old bull lost patience and charged toward the **errant** female. Running amongst her young, he slammed into the side of the cow's thigh with the long curved section of his nasal horn. She squealed in pain and surprise. The back part of her body was thrown to one side and she fell onto one of her own calves. She scrambled to her feet, but the unfortunate youngster was injured. It cried out as it tried to drag itself after mother and siblings. They did not seem to notice. They ran to catch up with the rest of the herd. But the cries did not go unheard. As the bull disappeared into the trees, a pair of *Troodon* moved in to silence the baby forever. Nature does not allow its young to suffer long.

With each passing day, the herd grew as it was joined by other groups of ceratopsians. The old bull continued to walk at the back of the growing herd. The bull was no longer **aggressive** towards other males. He mingled freely with the bulls that came in with the other herds, and even with the young males of the bachelor herds. Other species of ceratopsians, and even a few hadrosaurs, merged into the moving mass of flesh, but usually departed within a few days.

Once started, the push south became relentless. The herd was so big now that those at the front of the broad column could no longer see those at the back, even when the ground was moist enough to hold down the dust. Food was scarce, especially for those at the rear. Many of the young, weakened by the long days of walking, fell behind. If they could avoid the heavy footfalls of the bulls, they were free to spread out and find food amongst the trampled vegetation. A few of these stragglers regained enough strength to catch up with the herd when it stopped at the end of the day. Fewer still managed to survive until they could join other herds passing through the same region. For the majority, it was death — bitten in half by gigantic tyrannosaurs, or ripped apart by packs of dromaeosaurs.

The carnivores were moving south too. They were following herds of ceratopsians or hadrosaurs, ready to pick off those unfortunate enough to fall behind. As the migration continued, fewer of the young straggled behind the herd. The work of the carnivores now became more dangerous. They had to try to drag down old bulls and females weakened by the long march. Most of these older animals were still vigorous. Only a combined effort by a tyrannosaur pack could bring them down.

Such hunts were often risky. A predator could be fatally wounded by a great horned dinosaur fighting for its life.

The carnivores did not always have to risk their lives. In such a large migration, it was inevitable that some individuals would be injured. A young one could be stepped on, or an adult might slip sideways off a river bank. The carnivores rarely failed to take advantage of the opportunity to **prey** on these weakened animals. They were quick to put the injured out of their misery.

One day, the herd crossed the wide sandy bottom of a shallow river. The animals at the front of the herd waded across without any problem. But as more and more animals churned up the floor of the river, the sand and mud became saturated with water. The water, sand and mud combined to create a thick muck that became more and more difficult to wade through. Some of the great beasts began to sink into the quicksand and were unable to get out. Still, the unstoppable herd pushed on from behind.

The herd could easily circle around one or two stranded animals and leave them behind. But eventually so many became mired that the press of animals from behind started to climb right over top of the struggling creatures. Panicking as other ceratopsians stepped on their backs and forced them deeper into the mud, they flashed their great nasal horns upwards to pierce the bodies of their tormentors. Yet the herd continued to cross the small river over a bridge of their dead or dying comrades. The patch of mud was not large, but by the time the last animals had crossed, the herd was smaller by several hundred.

The days were now shorter, but at this latitude the sun was higher in the sky during the day. Vegetation was more abundant, having had all summer to recover from the spring migration north. Still the herd pushed on. A few days after crossing the quicksand, Twister noticed storm clouds gathering in the west. By late afternoon, torrential rain was falling. It beat down the vegetation that had not already been trampled by the herd, and turned the forest floor into a quagmire. The water darkened their hides, washing off dust and layers of dried skin to reveal the subtle color patterns of their flanks. Wave after wave of ceratopsians continued on in silent misery until darkness fell. In the morning, after spending an uncomfortable night huddled together for warmth, the herd set off once again.

The rain was very unusual for this time of year. A steady drizzle continued day after day. Occasionally, the drizzle became a downpour. The sky seemed to split open releasing enormous quantities of wind driven water. Of course the horned dinosaurs could not complain, but most of them felt the warmth draining from their bodies. They plodded onward even though they were beginning to lose strength. The strenuous journey was taking its toll. Many bones could now be seen under their hides. The smaller individuals felt hungry all the time. They tried eating as often as possible during the day, ripping off the lower branches of bushes as they walked. But they were expending more energy than they were taking in.

Finally, the fifth morning dawned with a clear sky. As the sun's warming rays penetrated the forest canopy, the centrosaurs rose to their feet to greet the day. There was no change in their routine, but the young were much more lively now that the sun shone. They ran circles around the adults, butting each other playfully in mock battle.

Wild river crossing

At mid-day, the herd climbed the **levee** of a wide but normally calm river. They pushed through the dense vegetation along the crest of the levee and looked across a huge expanse of rushing water. The days of rain had transformed the gentle river into a swollen giant. The water was thick and brown with its suspended load of mud and sand. Branches and even tree trunks were carried swiftly past them, indicating the strength of the current. The centrosaurs at the head of the column halted their march, intimidated by the dangerous waters. But the animals behind continued to push through the trees and brush. The leading animals were forced into the water. The waters were slower in this spot because of a bend in the river, so the leaders were able to strike out for the opposite shore with little trouble.

More and more animals plunged into the water, following the strongly swimming leaders. By now, the herd had spread along a wide front, and as many as a hundred animals were entering the water at the same time. Upstream, the banks had been undercut by the raging waters, and were no longer stable. The unsteady bank collapsed as the multi-tonne dinosaurs approached the water's edge. Falling no more than a body length, they nevertheless disappeared momentarily beneath the surface. Being naturally buoyant, they resurfaced quickly. But many came up beneath the legs and bodies of their comrades, who struggled to maintain their positions on top.

The young instinctively swam on the downstream side of the adults whenever possible. This afforded them some protection from the powerful current. However, there were more juveniles than adults, and those that entered the current alone were carried downstream as they struggled towards the opposite bank. Some tired quickly, and turned back towards the shore from which they had come. As they returned to the bank, many of the young were pushed underwater by the centrosaurs who were jumping, falling, or being pushed into the river. Exhausted from their short swim and winded by the great bodies that fell on them from above, many of the juveniles sank into the muddy depths never to be seen again. Those young that were carried downstream far enough past the herd were able to scramble back to shore, usually far from where they had entered the river.

Twister was on the upstream side of the group when he emerged from the dense brush on the levee. He stopped abruptly and looked across the confusion of water, floating debris, bodies, and wildly thrashing ceratopsians. Suddenly, one of the cows was pushed against his thigh by a pair of larger animals scrambling up the crest. Twister could only resist for an instant before his feet slipped off the edge. Sliding unceremoniously on his side down the bank, he plunged into the water tail first. His nose and mouth sank beneath the waters. Before he had a chance to resurface, he felt a mind-numbing jolt as the female fell on his head, pushing him deeper beneath the surface. Kicking wildly, she separated herself from Twister, smashing the bone beneath his left eye in her frantic struggle. Breaking surface, he painfully gulped down a mouthful of air while his legs sought desperately to touch the bottom. Another body plunged into the water, crashing against his left hip, and forcing him briefly underwater again. Legs and tail now worked in unison to push him away from the shore, where he was able to regain his breath.

Twister swam hemmed within a living raft of ceratopsians. The herd was united by the single purpose of reaching the opposite shore. More than once he felt his neighbors' legs push against his own, disrupting all chance of maintaining a consistent swimming rhythm. At one point the group became so densely packed that he had to stop kicking, and rest his head on the backs of the two animals directly in front of him. Close to the edge of the raft, he saw the giant trunk of an uprooted tree bearing down on them. There was nothing he could do except watch the log smash into the flank of his neighbor. That unfortunate animal expelled the air from its lungs with a groan and slipped under Twister's legs. Pushed by the log from behind, Twister was spun around so that his nose faced upstream. The tangled roots of the log snared one of the young ceratopsians behind him, but fortunately the bulk of the tree rotated away from him. Still being carried downstream by the current, Twister turned his nose towards the shore again, no longer entirely sure which bank of the river he was swimming towards.

It was a little more open here, and for a few moments Twister was able to swim strongly. Twice he felt large floating objects bump into his legs underneath the surface. Looking upstream he saw one of the young being carried by the current towards him. With a look of panic and desperation in its eyes, it attempted to scramble up onto Twister's back. Not expecting this move, the young bull panicked as he felt the back end of his body being pushed downwards. Adrenaline surged through his body, triggering quick action. He turned his great head swiftly and pushed the youngster off his back. Freed again, he made one last desperate attempt to reach the shore.

Finally, Twister felt the riverbed beneath his feet. He dragged himself into the shallow, quiet water on an inside bend of the river. Other ceratopsians stood and lay in the shallows, too exhausted to proceed. The carcasses of more animals welled up from beneath the surface, lifelessly bumping into the legs of the living. A small, vertical bank separated the shallows where they were standing from the heavily vegetated levee beyond. The exhausted animals packed against this steep bank. Some tried to scramble up the muddy bank only to slip backwards onto the others below. Farther downstream the banks were more gently sloped. The centrosaurs there were emerging from the water, easily climbing the bank and disappearing into the vegetation. But none of the animals with Twister considered going back into the river to follow the others. For now they stayed on their narrow strip of mud trapped by the steep bank on one side and the treacherous water on the other.

Twister lay down at the edge of the water. He watched the flow of animals downstream gradually thin out as the living climbed the banks and the dead were carried away by the flood waters. Looking down the narrow beach, he could see seven other individuals that were still alive. There were four females, two juveniles and one baby. Three dead centrosaurs lay on their sides slightly upstream.

Several hours passed while the animals rested. Slowly, the horrors of the river crossing began to fade. The sun broke through a hole in the clouds and warmed their bodies. Birds were singing in the bushes up above, oblivious to the disaster they had just witnessed.

In spite of the sunshine, the scene at the edge of the river was gruesome. One of the females near Twister lay close to the bank, breathing heavily. Her leg was twisted under her body at an unnatural angle, the result of a failed attempt to reach the top of the nearly vertical mud face. She had been further injured when a juvenile centrosaur fell on her chest. She would not last much longer.

The river current continued to jostle the carcasses of the dead animals at the water's edge. As gases built up in their abdomens, several of the bodies rolled onto their sides. The gory work of dismembering the carcasses had begun. Crocodiles, dwarfed by the bulk of the adult bodies, were violently tearing off strips of flesh, making the half submerged bodies rock up and down. Several types of birds, one with tiny sharp teeth, pecked holes through the thick hides to get at the red meat inside. All up and down the river, giant pterosaurs were swooping down from the skies. Their long, sharp beaks thrust deep into the bodies, pulling out organs and entrails which they swallowed whole. In spite of the richness of the feast, squawking disputes erupted periodically as the birds competed for the tastiest morsels. Most ominous, however, was the sound of the tyrannosaurs. Across the river and slightly downstream, several of these beasts were already at work.

Twister, like all the others of his kind, was not a great thinker. But a dinosaur did not have to be overly intelligent to be uncomfortable with this situation. As the shadows lengthened and the sky reddened, hunger began to overtake him. But what to do? What to do? He rose several times and walked around the narrow strip of mud that was their prison. As night fell, he settled down next to the other survivors. There was something comforting about physical contact with other living creatures.

Even so, Twister was unable to sleep. The horrible sounds of meat being devoured continued through the night — bones being crunched and broken, flesh being ripped and bolted, and the occasional eruption of tempers as scavenging **theropods** scuffled amongst themselves.

A new leader

Sunlight struck the upper levels of the trees, and trickled down the trunks until the rays finally fell on the surface of the river. The exhausted, hungry ceratopsians could see that the level of the river had dropped. The sky, pinkish in the east, was deep blue overhead. Mist rose from the river, but quickly burned away as the sun rose higher. The day soon grew warm, and the humidity became oppressive. Foul odors permeated the air, irritating the sensitive nostrils of the horned animals. The bloated carcasses of dead animals were occasionally swept away from the river banks and drifted past them. Partially eaten bodies could be seen stranded on every sandbar and pointbar. Theropods of all sizes were everywhere. Their territorial natures were forgotten as they came from far and wide, drawn by the stench of death. Many were stretched out sleeping on the ground, their bellies distended by the orgy of feeding.

Twister looked at the scene of carnage. At the edge of the low cliff, he saw the female with the broken leg; her eye stared lifelessly back at him. He turned and gazed at his remaining companions. They were weak from shock and hunger, but were otherwise fit. Suddenly, something happened deep inside

Twister's small brain. Twister was a young male just coming into the prime of his life. He had grown large and strong over the summer, but he had never before assumed the role of leader. He had never needed to look out for anyone except himself. But somehow the crisis of the river crossing had changed all that. Twister stood up and did what instinct urged him to do. With an angry bellow, he stood and shook his great head. Two of the females rose, and looked expectantly at him. The other four animals also raised their heads to stare at him. Twister was puzzled, both by his strange new feelings and by the reactions of the females to his behavior.

Pawing the mud and snorting, he turned suddenly and headed for the downstream side of their mud strip. Without pausing he plunged into the water. The current swept him close to the cliff that had imprisoned them. Turning his head, he saw that the others were following him. Twister swam with the current and before long, he felt the muddy bottom of the river. He walked up onto another point of land. The plants here were flattened from yesterday's high water, their mud-covered crowns pointing downstream.

The other centrosaurs followed Twister onto the shore. It was clear that they now looked to him for leadership. The seven animals passed between several partially eaten bodies. The haunches had been devoured by tyrannosaurs, and the guts were torn open by pterosaurs and small theropods. An enormous *Quetzalcoatlus* was startled by their arrival. His head had been thrust so deep into one body that he had been unaware of their approach. His belly too full to launch himself, he simply spread his wings and squawked loudly at them.

A little farther on, a **Gorgosaurus** suddenly reared up from behind another carcass. He had been sleeping, but awoke when he heard the ceratopsians approach. His hideous face was caked with mud and dried blood, and his teeth flashed as he issued a warning. However, the ceratopsians had little to worry about. This predator was well fed and did not show any interest in their presence. Detouring widely, the group moved closer toward the heavy vegetation on the crest of the levee. As the last of them passed the big theropod, he turned back towards the carcass, tore off another tremendous mouthful of flesh, groaned and settled back onto the ground.

The view that met their eyes as the centrosaurs passed over the crest of the levee was unexpected. The low-lying region beyond was flooded. There had been a breach in the river bank and many carcasses had been carried through this break out onto the flooded plain. There were more theropods here, but none showed much interest in the living ceratopsians. Although they were hunters most of the time, the easy availability of so much fresh meat had dulled their predatory nature.

After slogging through deep mud and water, the group topped another crest. Finally, they came to a region where the plants were not covered and choked by mud. A myriad of flowers bloomed on the ground and high into the trees. Birds were singing, and now that the sun was high in the sky the strident sound of katydids cut the silence. The horned dinosaurs followed Twister's lead, and stopped to feed. They remained there until the next day and slept more easily that night.

By morning, the ordeal of the river crossing was largely forgotten. But not entirely. Periodically a northeast breeze would carry the sickening stench of decaying flesh. Choking on a mouthful of food, Twister started to move rapidly south as though to escape this last reminder of the incident. The others followed without hesitation. Entering a clearing, Twister found himself suddenly face to face with a pair of tyrannosaurs. They were immature, and their long legs and lightly built frames hinted at speed and agility. They had been moving as rapidly as Twister, but in the opposite direction, attracted by the strong odors that advertised a free meal. Having travelled a great distance, they were hungry and ornery. Quickly, they separated and came towards the larger, heavier ceratopsian from both sides. Just before the tyrannosaurs reached him, the six other centrosaurs burst from the woods. The great hunters stopped in their tracks. While the tyrannosaurs hesitated, Twister moved fast. By the time the theropod on the right looked back at his prey, it was too late. Twister was in full charge.

The giant horn on Twister's nose caught the predator just above his left knee. Knocked painfully off balance, the theropod was able to recover fast enough to avoid being hit a second time. Turning quickly, the tyrannosaur disappeared into the vegetation with a noticeable limp. Twister turned towards the other carnivore, just in time to see it leap out of the path of a charging female centrosaur. As the angry female charged, the young centrosaurs in the group scrambled to get out of her way. The long sharp horn on her nose thrust upwards towards the tyrannosaur's belly as she ran by. Missed! Twisting in her tracks she thrust again. This time she was partially successful. The theropod had brought one of his heavily clawed feet onto the top of her head as he leaned over, attempting to bite her unprotected spine. But his reach was not long enough, and her horn dug into the calf of his leg. With a shriek of pain and annoyance, the tyrannosaur pulled back and moved off into the woods. The odor of decay, still heavy in the air, promised a much easier meal. The tyrannosaurs quickly forgot about the small group of ceratopsians.

Twister walked over to the female that had led the charge. After a quick inspection for injuries, he rubbed his nasal horn against hers. Although she turned away at first, he persisted until she eventually seemed to accept his advances. With that, they turned south again and walked for the rest of the day.

The little group now found itself in a region of lush vegetation. Here they stayed. The days grew shorter and a few of the nights were chilly. But here they were much farther south and the temperature remained generally moderate. With an abundance of food, the ceratopsians regained some of the weight and strength they had lost during the long trek from the North. Over the next few days, the horn rubbing ceremony was repeated several times. As the moon went into full phase, Twister had found a mate.

Spring

Several months later, Twister was quietly chewing the remains of a fern when he heard something running through the bushes. The footfalls were light but rapid, and he knew it was one of the small theropods. These small beasts were no threat to him and he normally would have ignored their presence. But today he had a deeply disquieting feeling. After a moment's pause, he suddenly turned and ran crashing through the underbrush. For the first time, Twister was protecting a nesting area.

Twister burst into the clearing where the eggs lay in their nests, only days away from hatching. A pair of *Troodon* was standing over one of the nests. One of the great eggs had been broken open, and a tiny but struggling centrosaur hung by its tail from the predator's mouth. The second *Troodon* was groping inside the pile of vegetation looking for another egg when Twister appeared. Startled by the sudden arrival of the charging ceratopsian, the *Troodon* dropped the embryo onto the soft pile of nesting material. Leaping to either side of the path between the nests, the troodontids easily evaded Twister's charge and moved to the edge of the clearing. The victim of the forced hatching rolled upright on the nest, its new eyes blinking in the bright light. The tiny beak nuzzled into the nesting material, and picked up some of the half decomposed vegetation. He was soon chewing happily, apparently unconcerned about the wounds halfway up its tail where the *Troodon* had bitten into it. He seemed unaware that he had been forced from his shell a few days early.

Twister lay down beside his newborn son. The *Troodon* crouched at the edge of the clearing, as if waiting for another opportunity. Soon the females returned to the nesting area. They had been feeding some distance away when they heard Twister's bellow. As the females came into the clearing, the two predators faded into the bushes. They would be back because they knew there would be more opportunities to feed here. But for now the nests were safe.

There were three nests to be tended, each a low mound of decomposing vegetation. The one **hatchling** seemed content enough, but his presence stimulated a protective reaction in the adults and they would not leave the area now. Under normal

circumstances, the eggs would all hatch within a day or two, even though they were laid over a much longer period.

Two days later, the first born was walking on its unsteady legs around the edge of the nest. It was then that another tiny head thrust itself from the vegetation, causing a stir of excitement amongst the adults. An hour later, several more tiny forms were wriggling on the surface. They had short faces, enormous eyes, and the frills at the back of their skulls were so short that they hardly covered any of the neck. Probing into the nests with their muzzles, the females could hear tiny voices from within several of the remaining eggs. Gently, they broke the shells of these, releasing their tiny offspring. A few of the round eggs were left unhatched. These had a certain odor and color that indicated there was no life inside. By the end of the day, almost forty babies were eating the nesting material and eggshells. The three females spread out around the edge of the nesting area, and lay down for the night. Twister stood, a proud father watching his family.

The babies grew and gained strength each day. Less than half of them would survive before the next long migration began. Such is Nature's way. As Twister watched over his small herd, the restlessness he had often felt during his bachelor years was replaced by a feeling of contentment. He was now a mature bull with a herd of his own. A new cycle had begun.

WHAT DO WE KNOW ABOUT *Centrosaurus*?

Introducing *Centrosaurus*

Centrosaurus was one of a very successful group of **herbivorous** (plant-eating) dinosaurs known as the ceratopsians, or horned dinosaurs. Fossil remains from more than twenty species of ceratopsians have been found, mostly in North America and Asia. Ceratopsians were quadrupedal animals (they walked on four legs). Most were bigger than cows, horses or even rhinoceroses. Ceratopsians have the largest skulls known for any land animal — up to three meters (ten feet) long. The front of the mouth was undoubtedly covered by a horny beak, giving it a parrot-like appearance. The large triangular skull extends backwards as a frill or shield over the neck. The frill can be ornamented in different ways, depending on **species**, age or sex. It has been suggested that the frill and horns were used for protection from tyrannosaurs, but they were probably also useful for attracting mates, scaring off rivals, and for identifying each other.

Centrosaurus apertus was first described in 1904 by Lawrence M. Lambe, using skull material found in Alberta. It is similar to *Triceratops*, but is more closely related to *Pachyrhinosaurus* and *Styracosaurus*, both of which are also from Alberta.

Like all ceratopsians, *Centrosaurus* is most easily recognized by characteristics of the adult skull (illustration Page 48). The horn over the nose is large, whereas those over the eyes are very short. The back of the frill is notched near the center. A pair of small horns face each other on either side of this notch. A larger pair of forward-facing horns slopes downward from the top of the frill in the adults. Usually one of these horns is larger than the other. Small bones (epoccipitals) along the sides of the frill give it a scalloped appearance. In the closely related *Styracosaurus*, some of these small bones have developed into long, straight spikes that fuse to the frill.

Baby centrosaurs look quite different than the adults. The horns over the nose and eyes are small nubbins of bone. The frill at the back of the skull is very short, and has no horns or epoccipitals. Because there are none of the distinctive features that are obvious in the adults, it would have been difficult to distinguish between the babies of *Centrosaurus*, *Pachyrhinosaurus* and *Styracosaurus*.

So many fossils of *Centrosaurus* have been discovered that it has become one of the best known ceratopsians. Even skin impressions have been known since 1917. The skin is made up of small and large tubercles, or bumps. The shape of each bump is similar to the shape of a stop sign. The bumps are all about the same thickness and they fit together like puzzle pieces. In many ways, the pattern on the skin is similar to the thick hide of the white rhinoceros.

Outcrop, *Centrosaurus* bonebed, Dinosaur Provincial Park. (Photograph by Philip Currie.)

We do not exactly know what *Centrosaurus* ate, but its teeth are clearly those of a herbivore. Studies done in Dinosaur Provincial Park (Alberta, Canada) show that 75 million years ago, there were diverse plants with at least 130 different species. These ranged in size from small herbs to bushes and big trees. Grass has never been found fossilized in Upper Cretaceous rocks. Presumably, centrosaurs were eating other plants as nutritious as grass is today.

Centrosaurus Bonebeds

Bonebeds form when the bones of many different animals are buried and fossilized in the same place. Sometimes whole skeletons are found in bonebeds, but usually the bones are completely mixed up. Bonebeds can form in many different ways. For example, when bones are washed out of river banks, they fall to the bottom of the river where they are concentrated into a single layer. If this layer gets buried and fossilized, it becomes a bonebed. Some of the bones may have been trapped in the river banks for thousands of years before falling to the bottom of the river, and they get mixed up with the remains of more recent animals. Most bonebeds found in Dinosaur Provincial Park have a mixture of bones from many different dinosaur species, and are called multigeneric bonebeds.

A small number of bonebeds are dominated by one single species of animals. These bonebeds represent unusual events that happened within very short periods of time. Usually, they form as the result of natural catastrophes (such as floods, fires, and volcanic eruptions). When one species dominates a bonebed, it is called a *monospecific* (or paucispecific) bonebed.

The first *Centrosaurus* bonebed (Quarry 143) was reported to one of us (Currie) in 1977 by two naturalists in Dinosaur Provincial Park. Photographs in the archives of the American Museum of Natural History (New York) show that the site was visited by Barnum Brown in 1913. Brown did not get around to working on the site, so the excavation had to wait 65 years. Once started, it continued for more than twelve years. It was the perfect site to

Centrosaurus bonebed, Dinosaur Provincial Park. (Photograph by Eva Koppelhus.)

work on, because most of the rock had eroded away to expose so many fossils that it was impossible not to step on bone. The bone layer is approximately 20 cm deep, and the original *Centrosaurus* bonebed covers an area half as big as a football field. There are between 20 and 60 bones per square meter. The vast majority of the bones come from only one species — *Centrosaurus apertus*.

Many other *Centrosaurus* bonebeds have been found in Dinosaur Provincial Park, and the Royal Tyrrell Museum of Palaeontology almost always

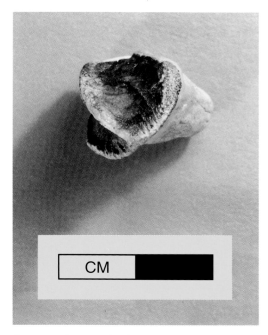

Ceratopsian tooth. (Photograph by Lawrence Dohy.)

has an excavation underway on at least one of them. Most of these bonebeds are deposited at approximately the same level in Dinosaur Park.

The dozen *Centrosaurus* bonebeds in Dinosaur Provincial Park are very important because they give us clues about how these animals lived and died. Because so many animals apparently died in the same places at the same time, it seems likely that they were living together in herds. The bonebeds include bones from babies, half-grown individuals and adults. There is enough variation amongst the adults to suggest that there were both males and females. The presence of young animals in the herds suggests that the adults were looking after their young.

In addition to dinosaur palaeontologists, many other scientists have been studying the centrosaur bonebeds. These studies help us to get as much information as possible about the environments where the dinosaurs lived and died. Geologists study the rocks to determine how the specimens were buried and fossilized, how old the rocks are, and what the physical environment was like. Palaeobotanists study the pollen, spores, leaves and wood to see which plants were living in the region 75 million years ago. Other biologists and palaeontologists study details of the anatomy of *Centrosaurus*, and the animals that lived with it. With all this information from many different types of scientists, we are able to piece together a picture of what life might have been like for the centrosaurs that lived millions of years ago.

Quarry 143 provides evidence that an absolute minimum of 80 *Centrosaurus* died at the same time. Only a quarter of the bonebed was excavated, and a lot of the bonebed had eroded away before it was discovered. This suggests that hundreds of animals had perished. And if the bonebed is connected with the other *Centrosaurus* bonebeds in Dinosaur Park, the number of dead animals represented could run into the thousands. Why would they herd in such large groups? One of the most common reasons that animals herd today is to migrate to regions where food is abundant only at certain times of the year. There are advantages to travelling in large groups, such as protection from predators. This strategy works most of the time. It insures that the maximum number of animals survive a migration, but sometimes there are catastrophes.

The skeletons in the bonebeds had fallen apart, and the bones were mixed up. *Centrosaurus* bones make up more than 85% of the bonebed composition. The crowns of theropod teeth are the next most common element. The discovery of many shed carnivore teeth in the same area is usually a good indication that the meat-eaters were feeding there. Theropods replaced their teeth every few years for as long as they lived, and loose teeth usually fell out when they were feeding. This conclusion is confirmed by the presence of tooth-marks on many of the ceratopsian bones.

There are other explanations for the accumulations of bones, and all need to be given careful consideration. For example, what if the myth of an "elephants' graveyard" actually had a prehistoric counterpart? Perhaps all the old *Centrosaurus* went to the same place when they were ready to die. However, the evidence does not seem to support this theory. Geological research suggests that each of the *Centrosaurus* bonebeds formed over a very short period of time, less than a few months. Furthermore, most of the

Centrosaurus horn. (Photograph by Eva Koppelhus.)

animals represented in the bonebed were not old when they died. Many, in fact, were juveniles. These facts do not agree with the idea of a special area where old animals went to die.

The most widely accepted explanation for the accumulation of bones in Quarry 143 is that a herd of *Centrosaurus* was **decimated** when they tried to cross a river in flood. Hundreds, or perhaps even thousands, of animals died, although we have no way of knowing how many survived the catastrophe. An individual *Centrosaurus* was probably a good swimmer, but the presence of so many panicky animals in the river at the same time created a disaster. In the panic, many would have been pushed underwater and drowned. The carcasses were washed downstream, coming to rest on sand bars and along the edge of the river. There is ample evidence (the trampled and tooth-marked bones, and the shed theropod teeth) to show that the bodies were scavenged by theropods after death. The remaining flesh of the scavenged carcasses would have rotted, and the skeletons would have fallen apart. The next time the river went into flood, it mixed up and buried the bones in sand and mud. The buried bones were fossilized, and the sediments turned into sandstone and mudstone.

Mass death events are not uncommon even today. There are many historical and archaeological records of bison herds being decimated by natural catastrophes, and the mass deaths of migrating wildebeest have been witnessed many times. In 1985, 10,000 caribou drowned in northern Quebec (Canada) when they tried to cross a river in flood. Still, ninety percent of that caribou herd did survive. At one point in our story, many centrosaurs died when they became bogged down in quicksand and were trampled by their own comrades. This is based on a true incident in which hundreds of bison (American Buffalo) perished in a small patch of quicksand at the edge of a river in South Dakota. If mammals with their large brains are incapable of avoiding such disasters, it is not surprising that dinosaurs occasionally had similar problems.

Centrosaurus skull. (Illustration by Jan Sovak.)

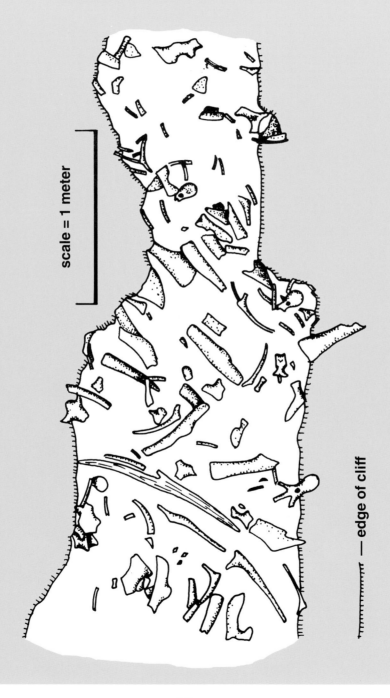

Centrosaurus bonebed, Dinosaur Provincial Park.
(Schematic by Philip Currie.)

scale = 1 meter

— edge of cliff

What Else Can We Guess About *Centrosaurus*

Appearance

We do not know what colors dinosaurs were. However, the presence of large eyes, large optic control centers in the brain, and flamboyant display structures like frills, crests, and horns suggests that dinosaurs relied heavily on their sense of sight. Because the closest relatives of dinosaurs are birds, which can be extremely colorful, a good case has been made by some scientists who believe that many dinosaurs were brightly colored.

Twister is the name we gave to one of the young *Centrosaurus* bulls. He was called Twister because the right side of his frill was distorted from an injury received when he was young. We have found twisted, asymmetric frills in the centrosaur bonebeds of Alberta. The frills and horns went through growth spurts when centrosaurs became "teenagers", and any injuries received before that would have been magnified. The more serious the injury to the growth centers, the more distorted the results.

Enemies

Daspletosaurus was a close relative of *Tyrannosaurus rex*, but was slightly smaller. It is more massive than *Albertosaurus*, and there is some evidence to suggest that it preyed mostly on horned dinosaurs like *Centrosaurus*. Even so, it would be a foolish predator that would attempt to kill a healthy ceratopsian. They may have relied on surprising lone animals, or perhaps they waited for opportunities to take down small or feeble individuals.

Herding Behaviour and Migration

Ceratopsians and other large dinosaurs have been found in the North, and they would have lived within the Arctic Circle for at least part of the year. During the summer months, the sun shone for 24 hours every day, just as it does now. This encourages the growth of very nutritious plants. Animals will always adapt to take advantage of such a rich source of food. However, during the middle of winter there would have been no sunlight. The plants would have dropped their leaves and become dormant. Large animals like *Centrosaurus* may have collected into herds to move south where they could find enough food to survive. But come the spring, the great herds would have formed once more as the animals pushed north into the Arctic Circle again.

There are several incidents in the story suggesting that male ceratopsians were very competitive, and that the herds were highly structured at certain times of the year. It is not known whether this is the type of behavior practiced by *Centrosaurus*, but it is one of the options used by modern herding animals. The aggressive behavior of the bulls usually is characteristic only at certain times of the year.

Controlling Parasites

As is written in the story, centrosaurs may have been pestered by biting insects. Fossilized insects are often found inside pieces of amber–fossilized resin or sap from trees. Biting flies related to black flies, sand flies and no–see–ums are very common in the 75 million year old amber of Alberta. They were no bigger than their modern relatives, but along with mosquitoes, ticks and other biting invertebrates, they probably made some days very miserable for dinosaurs.

Birds were common and diverse by the Late Cretaceous, and it is not unreasonable to think that some species may have developed a mutually advantageous relationship with some dinosaurs. Modern bird species will remove and eat insects from the backs of rhinoceroses, and will even clean the teeth of living crocodiles. Although many of the Cretaceous birds were quite modern in appearance (some had crests of feathers, while the males of other species had fantastically long tail feathers), some were still primitive enough to have teeth in their jaws.

Keeping Warm

It is not known whether some or all dinosaurs were warm-blooded or cold-blooded. Given the extremes of latitude that dinosaurs lived in, they would have encountered snow periodically. Because of their large size, their body temperatures would probably have remained relatively stable, and a little snow would not have hurt even a cold-blooded ceratopsian.

Nesting

Dinosaur eggs and embryos have been found in many locations around the world. None can be identified as having been laid by *Centrosaurus*. However, primitive ceratopsians like *Protoceratops* are known to have been egg-layers, and it is assumed that larger ceratopsians like *Centrosaurus* also laid eggs. Ceratopsians like *Centrosaurus* would have been too heavy to brood their eggs by lying on them. We can only guess at the nature of their nests. Some modern large birds will cover their eggs with decomposing vegetation, which produces enough heat to incubate the eggs. Perhaps centrosaurs did the same thing.

In writing this story, we used our knowledge of ceratopsians and filled in the gaps with guesswork based on modern animals. With this information, we can attempt to bring *Centrosaurus* back to life. There may never be a Time-Machine to carry us back to the Cretaceous and see how close our dreams matched reality. But further excavation and study of ceratopsians will improve our understanding of these fantastic animals. Like detectives searching for clues, future generations of palaeontologists will unravel the mysteries of ceratopsian behavior. The more we understand, the more incredible all dinosaurs seem to be.

DINOSAURS THAT LIVED WITH *Centrosaurus*

Theropoda (meat-eating dinosaurs)
Chirostenotes
Daspletosaurus
Dromaeosaurus
Dromiceiomimus
Gorgosaurus
Ornithomimus
Saurornitholestes
Richardoestesia
Struthiomimus
Troodon
Ankylosauria (armored dinosaurs)
Edmontonia
Euoplocephalus
Panoplosaurus
Hadrosauridae (duck-billed dinosaurs)
Brachylophosaurus

Corythosaurus
Gryposaurus
Hypacrosaurus
Lambeosaurus
Maiasaura
Parasaurolophus
Prosaurolophus
Pachycephalosauria (dome-headed dinosaurs)
Gravitholus
Ornatotholus
Pachycephalosaurus
Stegoceras
Ceratopsia (horned dinosaurs)
Anchiceratops
Chasmosaurus
Leptoceratops
Styracosaurus

WHERE TO SEE ORIGINAL SPECIMENS OF *Centrosaurus apertus*:

American Museum of Natural History, New York, USA
Canadian Museum of Nature, Ottawa, Canada
Dinosaur Provincial Park, Brooks, Canada
Museo de Ciencia Natural, La Plata, Argentina
Royal Ontario Museum, Toronto, Canada
Royal Tyrrell Museum of Palaeontology, Drumheller, Canada
United States National Museum of Natural History (Smithsonian), Washington, D.C., USA
University of Alberta Geology Museum, Edmonton, Canada
Yale Peabody Museum of Natural History, New Haven, USA

Centrosaurus bonebeds can be visited at Dinosaur Provincial Park in Alberta, Canada.

FURTHER READING

Currie, P. J., and K. Padian, 1998. The Dinosaur Encyclopedia. Academic Press, San Diego. (869 pages)

Dodson, P., 1996. The Horned Dinosaurs. Princeton University Press, Princeton, New Jersey. (346 pages)

GLOSSARY

adrenaline: a hormone produced by the body that stimulates the heart.

aggressive: behaving with bold determination and readiness for conflict.

asymmetrical: not even, not the same on both sides.

carnivores: meat-eaters.

centrosaur: a popularized name for a subfamily of ceratopsian dinosaurs known as the Centrosaurinae. This subfamily includes *Achelousaurus*, *Centrosaurus*, *Einiosaurus*, *Pachyrhinosaurus* and *Styracosaurus*. Unlike *Triceratops* and its kin, centrosaurs have **short horns over the eyes and long horns over the nose.**

Centrosaurus: a genus of horned dinosaur (ceratopsian) from Alberta. First named by Lawrence Lambe in 1904.

ceratopsian: horned dinosaurs, including *Psittacosaurus*, *Protoceratops*, and *Triceratops*. Ceratopsians are characterized by the parrot-like beak, horns over the nose and/or eyes, and a frill that extends from the back of the skull out over the neck.

Daspletosaurus: a large theropod closely related to *Tyrannosaurus rex*. This massive animal seems to be most common at sites where there are lots of ceratopsians, which suggests that ceratopsians may have been its preferred food.

decimate: to kill a large part of a group.

dominant: superior to all others in power, importance.

errant: straying from the regular path or standard behaviour.

Gorgosaurus: a large theropod of the tyrannosaurid family, which also includes *Albertosaurus*, *Daspletosaurus* and *Tyrannosaurus rex*. *Gorgosaurus* is the most common tyrannosaur in Dinosaur Provincial Park (Alberta).

hatchling: All dinosaurs probably laid eggs, and more than 200 dinosaur egg sites are presently known. Newly hatched animals are often referred to as hatchlings.

herbivore: plant (herb) eating animals.

imperceptible: too slight or small to be aware of through the senses.

juveniles: juveniles are immature animals, usually about half grown.

latitude: the distance north or south from the earth's equator, measured in degrees.

levee: a levee is the naturally formed, high bank of a river. Levees usually control the course of a river that is close to sea-level, raising it above the level of the surrounding land like an aqueduct. If the water rises too high and ruptures the levee, the flood-waters will quickly flood all of the surrounding lowlands.

mammals: warm blooded animals that have hair covered bodies, and suckle their young.

migration: In its simplest form, "migration" can be defined simply as the movement of living things from one place to another. However, we usually think of migration as being the regular, scheduled movements of animals. For example, birds in the northern hemisphere fly north in the summer, and south in the winter.

ominous: threatening.

predator: a meat-eating animal that acquires most of its food by hunting and killing other animals.

prey: prey animals are those that are killed by predators for food. Usually the "prey" is a plant-eater.

species: a group of living organisms (plants or animals) that can produce offspring.

theropods: "beast foot" is the literal translation for "theropod", referring to its birdlike three toed feet. All meat-eating dinosaurs are theropods.

troodontids: All known troodontids were relatively small (man-sized) theropods that lived during Cretaceous times in the northern hemisphere. Troodontids had the largest brains known for any dinosaur. It was about six times the size of a crocodile brain, and was equivalent to the brains of many modern mammals and birds.

tyrannosaur: The Tyrannosauridae is a family of meat-eating dinosaurs that is known only from the Late Cretaceous of the northern hemisphere. Tyrannosaurs include some of the largest and most sophisticated theropods known, including *Albertosaurus*, *Alectrosaurus*, *Aublysodon*, *Daspletosaurus*, *Gorgosaurus*, *Tarbosaurus* and *Tyrannosaurus rex*. The forelimbs are reduced in size, and retain only two clawed fingers. Tyrannosaurs are more closely related to *Troodon* and *Ornithomimids* than they are to animals like *Allosaurus*.

vegetation: plant life.

velociraptors: are a group of relatively small, theropod dinosaurs that have adapted one of the claws on the feet into an enlarged killer claw that can disembowel its prey. Two of the best known velociraptors are *Velociraptor* and *Deinonychus*.